Regions of the United States: The Midwest

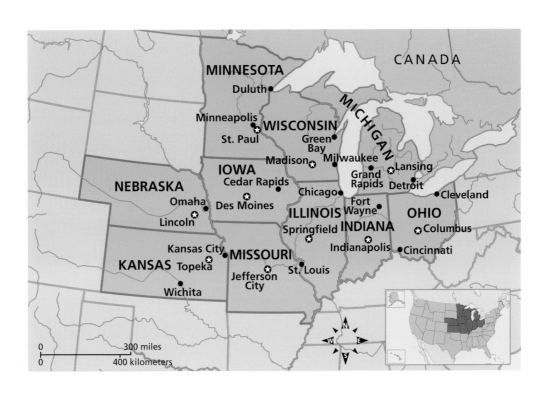

Judson and Elizabeth Curry

Chicago, Illinois

© 2006 Raintree
An imprint of Capstone Global Library, LLC
Chicago, Illinois

Customer Service 888-363-4266

Visit our website at www.heinemannraintree.com

Produced for Raintree by
White-Thomson Publishing Ltd.
Bridgewater Business Centre
210 High Street, Lewes, BN7 2NH

For information, address the publisher:
Raintree, 100 N. LaSalle, Suite 1200, Chicago, IL 60602

Edited by Susan Crean
Page layout by Clare Nicholas
Photo research by Amy Sparks
Illustrations by John Fleck
Printed and bound in the United States of America, North Mankato, Minnesota.
16 15 14
10 9 8 7 6 5 4
082014 008368RP

**Library of Congress
Cataloging-in-Publication Data**

Curry, Jud, 1964-
  The Midwest / Jud and Elizabeth Curry.
      p. cm. -- (Regions of the USA)
  Includes bibliographical references and index.
  ISBN 1-4109-2311-8 (hc) -- ISBN 978-1-4109-2319-6 (pb)
  1. Middle West--Juvenile literature. I. Curry, Elizabeth, 1966- II.
Title. III. Series.
F351.C88 2007
977--dc22

                              2006004698

012012   007070RP

Acknowledgments
The publisher would like to thank the following for permission to reproduce photographs:
pp. 4, 5, 6, 22, 32, 33, 35, 51B David Frazier; pp. 8, 9 Richard A. Cooke/Corbis; pp. 10-11, 13, 15, 17A, 17B, 19, 23, 24, 29,
36-37, 37B, 40, 41, 49, 51A Viesti Associates; p. 12, 26A Library of Congress; p. 16 Skjod Photographs/The Image Works; p.
18 Topfoto/The Image Works; 21A U.S. Fish and Wildlife Service; p. 20 David McFarlane/iStock; p. 21 Sascha Burard/iStock;
p. 25 Owen Franken/Corbis; p. 26B Jose Fuste Raga/Corbis; p. 27 Tannen Maury/The Image Works; pp. 28, 34 Gibson Stock
Photography; p. 30 Farrell Grehan/Corbis; p. 31 Joseph Sohm/The Image Works; pp. 39, 46 Richard Hamilton Smith/
Corbis; pp. 38, 50 Jeff Greenberg; p. 42 Foodpix/photolibrary.com; p. 43 Erik Kozlowski/iStock; pp. 44-45 Robin
Jerstad/Reuters/Corbis; p. 45A Topfoto; p. 47A Michael Westoff/The Image Works; p. 47B Tom Bean/Corbis;
p. 48 Layne Kennedy/Corbis.

Every effort has been made to contact copyright holders of any material reproduced in this book. Any omissions
will be rectified in subsequent printings if notice is given to the publisher.

Cover photo of Gateway Arch, St Louis, Missouri reproduced with permission of Viesti Associates

Contents

Some words are shown in bold, **like this.** You can find out what they mean by looking in the glossary.

The Midwest

State names

Of all the Midwest state names, only Indiana is not a Native American word, although Indiana does mean "land of Indians." Illinois is Algonquin for "tribe of superior men," while Iowa means "this is the place" or "beautiful land." Kansas is a name taken from the Kansa Indians, whose name means "people of the south wind." Michigan means "great water," while Minnesota means "sky-tinted water" and Missouri is an Iliniwek word meaning "owner of big canoes." Nebraska means "flat water," Ohio is an Iroquoian word meaning "great river," and Wisconsin is from a word that is thought to mean "gathering of waters."

Where could you go in the United States to find rolling hills, wide open fields, rugged shorelines, deep forests, shining lakes, mighty rivers, busy farms, and giant cities? In this region, the winter is cold and snowy and the summer is hot. Some of its lakes are so wide that they look like oceans and its prairies are so wide and flat that they appear to be seas of waving grass.

The Midwest is home to all of these things! The ten amazing states of the Midwest region contain more surprises than you might ever guess.

There are more than 18 miles (29 kilometers) of trails for running, walking, biking, and skating along Chicago's lakefront.

Just after the **American Revolution**, in the late 1700s, settlers began moving west into the land that is now called the Midwest. At that time, the Midwest formed the western edge of the United States. As **pioneers** kept moving even farther west these states were no longer part of the "west," instead, they became known as the Midwest.

The Midwest is also known as America's heartland, because of its position in the center of the United States, and the nation's "breadbasket," because of its large fields of wheat and other grains.

More than half the corn grown in Iowa is exported to other countries.
▼

Find out later...

On which river can this steamboat be found?

What does this painting portray?

What caused the strange rock formations found in the Wisconsin Dells?

Shape of the land

Glaciers, or giant sheets of ice, shaped much of the land in the Midwest. Glaciers have buried the Midwest at least four different times over the last million years. The most recent deep freeze that brought glaciers down over Wisconsin, Michigan, and Minnesota began about 70,000 years ago and ended just 10,000 years ago.

Midwest links

The Midwest is between the Allegheny Mountains to the east and the Rocky Mountains to the west. The Midwest serves as a **hub** for the United States. It links the East, South, and West together.

The ten states of the Midwest are located on both sides of the Mississippi River, with five states on each side of the river. The five Midwest states east of the Mississippi River are Ohio, Indiana, Michigan, Illinois, and Wisconsin. These states are also bordered by the Great Lakes. The Ohio River forms the southern **border** of Ohio, Indiana, and Illinois. The five Midwest states west of the Mississippi are Minnesota, Iowa, Missouri, Kansas, and Nebraska.

Farms such as this one in southern Wisconsin are a common sight throughout the Midwest.

Fact file

State	Population	Size
Illinois	12,419,293	57,918 sq. mi. (150,006 sq. km)
Indiana	6,080,485	36,420 sq. mi. (94,327 sq. km)
Iowa	2,926,324	56,276 sq. mi. (145,754 sq. km)
Kansas	2,688,418	82,282 sq. mi. (213,109 sq. km)
Michigan	9,938,444	96,810 sq. mi. (250,737 sq. km)
Minnesota	4,919,479	86,943 sq. mi. (225,181 sq. km)
Missouri	5,595,211	69,709 sq. mi. (180,545 sq. km)
Nebraska	1,711,263	77,358 sq. mi. (200,356 sq. km)
Ohio	11,353,140	44,828 sq. mi. (116,103 sq. km)
Wisconsin	5,363,675	65,503 sq. mi. (169,652 sq. km)

Land of promise

To the first pioneers, the Midwest was a land of promise, with good soil, forests full of trees for lumber and game for hunting, clear lakes full of fish, and many rivers to make travel swift and easy.

People and History

Nearly 2,000 years ago, people were already living in the Midwest region. Some of these groups lived along the Ohio River in what is now southern Ohio, Indiana, and Illinois. These people left no written records, so we know very little about their lives. We do not even know what they called themselves. **Archeologists** now call them the Adena and Hopewell tribes.

Adena culture

The Adena people first arrived in this part of the Midwest around 1000 B.C. Around this time, they developed ways to farm and began growing foods such as raspberries, strawberries, hazelnuts, and walnuts. The Adena people also made pottery.

Mica carvings

The Hopewell people carved flat shapes from thin sheets of **mica**. They got materials like mica through long-distance trade with other groups of people. They traded with people from as far away as the Atlantic Ocean, the Rocky Mountains, and the Gulf of Mexico.

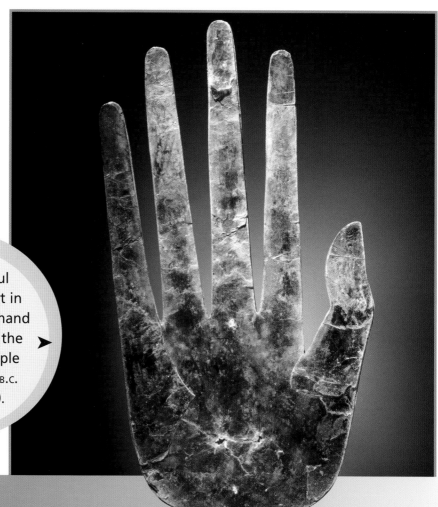

This beautiful mica ornament in the shape of a hand was carved by the Hopewell people between 100 B.C. and A.D. 350.

Hopewell culture

The Hopewell people began to appear in this area around 100 B.C. The Hopewell people were skilled artists who created beautiful ornaments, jewelry, and symbolic objects. The Hopewell culture seems to have died out mysteriously around A.D. 500.

Clues from the past

The Adena and Hopewell cultures did leave some mysterious clues. They built large mounds of earth. Some mounds were built to bury the dead. Other mounds may have been built for ceremonial reasons. Some mounds were 60 feet (20 meters) high and 300 feet (100 meters) wide.

Serpent Mound

An enormous snake-shaped mound can be found in Adams County in Ohio. It is about .25 miles (.4 kilometers) long and about 20 feet (6 meters) wide. Archeologists first believed this mound was constructed by the Adena people, who built other mounds in the area. However, more recent tests show that it was built by a later group of Native Americans, often called the Fort Ancient **culture**, around A.D. 1000.

From above, Ohio's Serpent Mound is clearly visible. You can see the snake's tail curled at one end and its body winding along the land.

Lewis and Clark Expedition

In order to explore the new Louisiana Territory, Captains Meriwether Lewis and William Clark and a small group of men traveled more than 8,000 miles (12,875 kilometers). Lewis and Clark began and ended their journey near St. Louis, where the Missouri and the Mississippi Rivers meet. The expedition took place between March 1804 and September 1806.

Moving west

Following the American Revolution, the land that we now call the Midwest was split between two countries. France controlled the territory west of the Mississippi River, while the lands east of the Mississippi were the Northwest Territory of the United States of America. The Northwest Territory later became the states of Ohio, Indiana, Michigan, Illinois, and Wisconsin.

The Louisiana Territory

In 1803 the United States purchased the Louisiana Territory from France. The **Louisiana Purchase** included the lands that would become the states of Minnesota, Iowa, Missouri, Kansas, and Nebraska.

St. Louis is thought of as the gateway to the West because so many settlers began their westward journey from this city. The stainless steel Gateway Arch is 630 feet (192 meters) high.

Homesteaders move in

In 1862 Congress passed the **Homestead Act**. According to this law, settlers could claim 160 acres of land, providing they built a house, planted crops, and lived there for five years. Many **homesteaders** headed west into the Great Plains, including the states of Kansas and Nebraska. These settlers included Swedish, Norwegian, German, Irish, and Russian **immigrants**.

Between 1860 and 1880, the number of African-American settlers in Kansas jumped from fewer than 1,000 to more than 40,000. African-American settlers accounted for about 5 percent of the Kansas population in 1880.

Laura Ingalls Wilder

Laura Ingalls Wilder, author of the *Little House* books, lived as a child with her homesteading family near Independence, Kansas. In fact, Laura Ingalls Wilder lived all around the Midwest. She was born in Wisconsin and grew up in Kansas, Minnesota, and Iowa. She and her husband, Almanzo Wilder, finally settled in Missouri.

The Underground Railroad

At the time of the Civil War (1861–1865) the "free states" of the Midwest had banned slavery. In fact, the Republican Party was formed in Ripon, Wisconsin, in the 1850s to oppose slavery in new territories.

The **Underground Railroad** was the name given to the dangerous journey taken by slaves as they escaped to freedom. On this "railroad" there were "conductors," ordinary people who helped escaping slaves. "Stations" were houses or other buildings where escaping slaves could rest safely. The Midwest was often a final destination for escaping slaves.

Dred Scott

Dred Scott and his wife Harriet were enslaved African Americans owned by a slaveholder from Missouri. In the 1830s, the Scotts were taken by their slaveholder to the free states of Illinois and Wisconsin. In 1846 Dred Scott sued for their freedom. Although the Scotts lost their suit in the Supreme Court and were never freed, their case was an important step toward the end of slavery.

This newspaper from 1857 shows Dred Scott, his wife Harriet, and their children, Eliza and Lizzie.

Missouri and Kansas

Missouri, unlike other Midwest states, was admitted to the United States as a state in which slavery was allowed. When the Civil War began, Missouri became one of the border states, split between the **Union** and the **Confederacy**. Often members of the same family would fight on different sides.

Even before the Civil War, Kansas was a battleground. Settlers who were in favor of slavery in Kansas fought bloody battles with those settlers who opposed slavery. In 1861, just months before the start of the Civil War, Kansas was admitted to the Union as a free state.

◄ This house in Springfield, Illinois, was home to Abraham Lincoln and his family from 1844 to 1861, before he became president. Illinois now calls itself the "Land of Lincoln."

Land in the Area

Great Lakes dunes

The sand dunes on the shores of the Great Lakes are the largest freshwater coastal dunes in the world. Beach dunes develop on low-lying shores of Lake Michigan and are mostly sand. Perched dunes, on the other hand, sit on a high **plateau** above the shore and are made up of sand and other materials.

A major feature of the Midwestern landscape can be found across the northeast part of the region. It is made up of vast expanses of water, which are not just ordinary lakes. They are the Great Lakes.

Lake Superior is the largest and deepest Great Lake. It covers 32,000 square miles (82,000 square kilometers) and has a maximum depth of 1,330 feet (405 meters). It is an important shipping route known for the beauty of its shoreline. Apostle Islands National Lakeshore, off the coast of Wisconsin, includes 22 islands and sandstone sea caves. Isle Royale National Park is a wild and beautiful island with wildlife such as wolves and moose. Although Isle Royale is part of the state of Michigan, it is closer to the coastlines of both Canada and Minnesota.

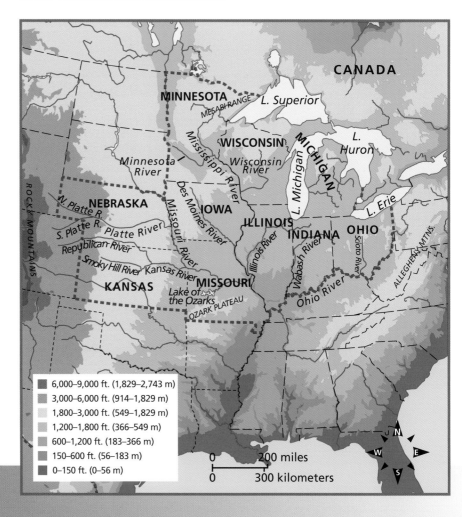

■	6,000–9,000 ft. (1,829–2,743 m)
■	3,000–6,000 ft. (914–1,829 m)
□	1,800–3,000 ft. (549–1,829 m)
□	1,200–1,800 ft. (366–549 m)
■	600–1,200 ft. (183–366 m)
■	150–600 ft. (56–183 m)
■	0–150 ft. (0–56 m)

0   200 miles

0   300 kilometers

Great Lakes

Lake Michigan is the only Great Lake entirely in the United States. The others are shared with Canada. Lake Michigan is the second deepest of the Great Lakes, with a maximum depth of 923 feet (281 meters). Lake Huron is connected to Lake Michigan by the Straits of Mackinac. Lake Erie is the shallowest of all the Great Lakes, with an average depth of 62 feet (19 meters). Lake Erie often freezes in the winter.

Arch Rock, located on Mackinac Island, is a natural limestone formation; it is 50 feet (15 meters) wide and rises 149 feet (45 meters) above the blue water of the Straits of Mackinac.

Mackinac Island

Mackinac Island, between Lake Michigan and Lake Huron, gets its name from a Native American word meaning "big turtle." This beautiful island is a popular tourist destination. After arriving by ferryboat, you must travel on foot, by bicycle, or by horse-drawn carriage, since no cars are allowed. Each year, sailboats race 335 miles (539 kilometers) from Chicago to Mackinac Island, the entire length of Lake Michigan.

Fact file

The Great Lakes contain 20 percent of all fresh water on Earth.

The Mississippi River

There are many important rivers throughout the Midwest, including the Ohio River and the Missouri River. However, the upper Mississippi River is the backbone of the Midwest.

The Mississippi River flows from northern Minnesota through the center of the Midwest region until it is joined by the Ohio River at the southern tip of Illinois. From there, the Mississippi River flows south toward the Gulf of Mexico.

The Mississippi River supports **commercial** navigation, as well as recreation, fish, and wildlife. It is also a **flyway** for 40 percent of North American waterfowl and shore birds.

Mississippi steamboat

In the late 1800s, steamboats regularly traveled up and down the Mississippi River, carrying freight and passengers. The author Mark Twain, whose real name was Samuel Clemens, described his experiences on a Mississippi River steamboat in his book *Life on the Mississippi* (1883).

The Delta Queen, docked on ➤ the Upper Mississippi in St. Paul, Minnesota, is a steam-powered riverboat.

Forests and caves

The Midwest is currently home to about 77 million acres (31 million hectares) of forest, though this is just a small part of the huge forests that greeted the first settlers. Oak and hickory forests are the most common type, followed by maple, beech, and birch forests. Northern Minnesota, Wisconsin, and Michigan have many large pine forests.

Hidden below the surface of the southern Midwestern states are caves of every size. Missouri alone has more than 5,700 caves. Most of these caves are formed from **limestone**, a kind of rock. Water seeps underground and slowly eats away at the rock, forming caves and caverns.

Porcupine Mountains Wilderness State Park, on the shore of Lake Superior in Michigan's Upper Peninsula, is a wild and beautiful place to camp or hike.
▼

Meramec Caverns

Caverns in Missouri housed escaped slaves fleeing along the Underground Railroad. The Meramec Caverns (above) also served as a gunpowder storage dump during the Civil War. They even provided a hideout for Jesse James, the bank robber and outlaw, in the late 1800s.

No one can change the weather, but sometimes the weather can change a city. In January 1979 a sudden blizzard may have changed the outcome of the Chicago mayoral election. Mayor Michael Bilandic was unseated by challenger Jane Byrne. Byrne won in part because Mayor Bilandic's city government was unable to keep Chicago streets plowed during the blizzard.

Surviving the cold

In the Midwest the weather is never boring. Weather in the Midwest includes hot summers and cold winters. The northern Midwestern states near the Canadian border experience cold and often snowy winters. States that border the Great Lakes often experience severe "lake-effect snow." This happens when cold winds blow across the lakes, collecting moisture that becomes snow.

In cities such as Minneapolis, Minnesota, where winters can be very cold and snowy, downtown buildings are connected by a system of second-floor walkways. These "skyways" or "pedways" allow pedestrians to walk for five miles (eight kilometers) without going outside.

Having fun in the snow is part of life in the Midwest in the winter.

Fact file

The snowiest part of the Midwest is the Upper Peninsula of Michigan. In an average winter, this area receives 9 feet 2 inches (2.8 meters) of snow.

Summer weather

Summertime in the Midwest ranges from wet and mild weather in southern Ohio, Indiana, and Missouri, to very cold weather in the north. Summers are dry in the west of Nebraska and Kansas. Some states in the Midwest face summers that include frequent heat waves and **drought**. Many farms in the Midwest, especially in Kansas and Nebraska, rely on **irrigation** systems to water crops during droughts.

Heat waves can be deadly for people in urban areas. "Heat islands" form because the buildings and pavements of a city hold the heat. Summer temperatures in cities are often 2–10 °F (2–6 °C) hotter than surrounding rural areas. In July 1995 a five-day heat wave with high temperatures between 94 and 106 °F (34 and 41 °C) caused the deaths of about 740 mostly poor or elderly people in Chicago.

Pedestrians can stay warm when the weather is cold by using the skyways in Minneapolis.

Twisting tornadoes

Remember the Kansas "twister" that carried away the house containing Dorothy and Toto in *The Wizard of Oz*? In fact, in an average year, Kansas experiences 48 tornados. Tornados form most often during the spring. The flat land of the Midwest allows cold, Canadian air to meet the warm, moist, tropical air that flows north from the Gulf of Mexico. As the warm and cold air swirl together, tornados can easily form.

19

Animals and Plants

Wild animals in the city

Many animals have adapted well to life in Midwestern cities and suburbs. Peregrine falcons, which usually nest on ledges or outcroppings of cliffs, have been found nesting on the window ledges of skyscrapers. Peregrines are fierce predators. They hunt common city birds such as pigeons and starlings, helping to control the population of these birds.

There are plenty of animals in the Midwest, and not all of them live on farms. The early inhabitants of the Midwest region found plentiful wildlife of all kinds. However, as the human population of the Midwest grew and forests and prairies were transformed into farmland, wild animals have faced many challenges.

White-tailed deer live in wooded areas throughout the Midwest. These deer rarely travel further than one square mile (2.6 square kilometers). Because of the increase in human population, white-tailed deer often find themselves sharing their **habitat** with people.

In the early 1900s, the number of white-tailed deer had dropped to 300,000. Now, however, there are more than 30 million white-tailed deer living in the United States.

Keeping bats safe

Indiana bats can be found in many Midwest states, including Indiana, Illinois, Missouri, and Kentucky. Unfortunately, because of human visitors to their cave homes, Indiana bats have become **endangered**, with fewer than 400,000 left in the world. Some caves now have special gates installed that allow bats in but keep people out of the caves.

The average lifespan of an Indiana bat is ten to twenty years.

Bison

Until the late 1800s, huge herds of bison roamed the plains of Nebraska and Kansas. However, by the end of the 1800s the bison herds had been reduced by overhunting from 30 million animals to very few.

Alien invaders

The Great Lakes have also become home to some uninvited guests. As ocean freighters from all over the world enter the Great Lakes from the Atlantic Ocean, they often carry fish and aquatic creatures who make themselves at home in the Great Lakes. Zebra mussels, sea lampreys, and alewives are all accidental additions.

Although some bison remain in the wild in protected areas, most bison currently live on private ranches and farms. These ranches and farms raise bison as livestock.

What happened to prairies?

In 1837 John Deere invented a steel-bladed plow that could break through the prairie **sod**, and since then nearly all the original Midwestern prairie has been converted to farmland. Before the arrival of European settlers, Illinois had 22 million acres (about 9 million hectares) of prairie; now, only 2,000 acres (800 hectares) remain, less than one-hundredth of one percent.

Trees and grass

Woodlands and prairies are the two most common plant **ecosystems** of the Midwest. Woodlands, dominated by trees, are most commonly found near rivers, streams, and other sources of water. In the drier prairies, grasses are the most common plants.

Prairie grasses have skinny leaves that lose less moisture, and their roots can grow 15 to 20 feet deep (4.5 to 6.1 m). Two kinds of prairies were once common in the Midwest. Tallgrass prairies covered two thirds of Illinois and almost all of Iowa. Mixed-grass prairies were most common in Kansas and Nebraska.

Settlers were astonished by the vast open expanses of the prairies. The endless waving grass reminded them of an ocean.

Oak savannas

In nearly every Midwest state, where prairies meet forests, you can find oak savannas. These areas have scattered black oak trees with a varied ground cover of herbs, grasses, and shrubs. Oak savannas are home to uncommon plants such as yellow pimpernel and false foxglove and birds such as the northern flicker.

In order to grow properly, oak savannas require occasional fires. Fires kill off the seedlings of other trees, keeping the area from becoming a forest. However, oak savannas have become an endangered ecosystem.

Farmland has replaced many oak savannas and prairies once found throughout the Midwest.

Natural wetland

Volo Bog in northern Illinois is a unique natural area. A bog is a **wetland** that is made of layers of dead plant material, often peat moss. The plants in Volo Bog grow on a mat of peat moss, which floats on a small, rain-fed lake. It is called a "quaking bog" because the trees that grow there shake and quiver when people or animals walk on the floating peat mat.

Cities and Towns

The Midwest has always been an important crossroads in the United States, where people from different cultures have come. The Midwest is becoming home to new ethnic groups all the time.

Land of immigrants

In the 1800s and 1900s, European immigrants came to Midwest cities. As Midwestern cities became centers for industry, African Americans from the southern states moved north to these cities, where factory jobs offered new opportunities. Most recently, individuals and families from Central and East Asia and Mexico have made the Midwest their home.

Cultural mix

One ethnic group that has recently arrived in the Midwest is the Hmong people. The Hmong are an Asian ethnic group whose homelands are in southern China, northern Vietnam, and Laos. St. Paul, Minnesota, has the largest urban concentration of Hmong anywhere in the United States. Minnesota State Senator Mee Moua is a Hmong American who was born in Laos.

Chicago's Chinatown features Chinese shops, restaurants, building styles, and cultural centers.

Midwest diversity

As immigrants move into Midwest cities, they often form their own neighborhoods, with churches, schools, and cultural life.

Midwestern cities and towns have had to adapt to each of the different groups of immigrants who have made the Midwest their home. In Garden City, Kansas, for example, signs are printed in English, Vietnamese, and Cambodian for the benefit of the many Southeast Asians who have come to Kansas to find factory work.

This small farmers' market in Minneapolis is run by mostly Hmong farmers living in Minnesota.

A cultural blend

In Pottsville, Iowa, some of the most recent arrivals are Lubavitcher Hasidic Jews. They arrived in 1988 from Brooklyn, New York, to open a kosher slaughterhouse. At first the religious and cultural differences between the people of Pottsville and the newly arrived Lubavitchers seemed great, but with time the two groups have come to understand and appreciate one another.

Chicago, Illinois

Chicago is by far the largest city in the Midwest, and the third-largest city in the United States, after New York and Los Angeles. Chicago started as a frontier town in 1833 with a population of 350.

The city population is now nearly 2.9 million, with more than 9 million people living in the extended **metropolitan area**. Chicago has been called one of the ten most culturally and economically influential cities in the world.

The Chicago Fire

On October 8, 1871, a raging fire started in Chicago (above). Some say that the fire began when Mrs. O'Leary's cow kicked over a lantern, but no one really knows the true cause. Whatever the cause, the fire raged until the morning of October 10, when rain began to fall. The fire burned 18,000 buildings, killed 300 people, and left almost 100,000 Chicago residents, one-third of the city's population, homeless.

Visitors to Chicago's Millennium Park get a new view of themselves and the skyline from their reflections in the Cloud Gate sculpture.

Midwest metro areas

The population of a city can be measured as the number of people living within the city itself or by the number of people living in the metropolitan area that includes the city and all surrounding suburbs.

After Chicago, Detroit, Michigan is the largest city in the Midwest, with more than 900,000 people, followed by Indianapolis, with a population just under 800,000. Detroit also has the second-highest metropolitan area population, with 5.5 million people. The Twin Cities of Minneapolis and St. Paul, Minnesota, however, have the third-highest metropolitan area population, with 3 million people.

Sears Tower, Chicago

The Sears Tower, the fourth tallest skyscraper in the world, rises to a height of 1,450 feet (442 meters) above the city of Chicago. The 110 stories of the Sears Tower contain an entire mini-city, with stores, apartments, and recreation facilities of all kinds.

On a clear day, it is possible to see 40 to 50 miles (64-80 kilometers) from the top of the Sears Tower. You can see four states: Illinois, Indiana, Wisconsin, and across the lake to Michigan.

Fact file

The people of the Midwest account for just over one-fifth of the entire United States population.

Midwest manufacturing

Many Midwestern cities, including Milwaukee, Detroit, and Cleveland, were once mighty centers of manufacturing. These cities grew and prospered during the first half of the 1900s as heavy industry expanded throughout the Midwest. However, since the 1960s, the steel and manufacturing industries have moved away from these cities.

Detroit, Michigan

Detroit, the largest city in Michigan and the seventh-largest city in the United States, was the site of Henry Ford's first Model T automobile plant in 1908. Detroit had the first paved concrete road and the first traffic light in the United States. As the home of the automobile, Detroit is often called the Motor City.

Located on the Detroit River between Lake Erie and Lake St. Clair, Detroit is an important gateway between the United States and Canada and a busy center for international shipping, receiving freighters from more than 100 international ports.

Downtown Detroit can be viewed from across the Detroit River, in Canada.

Milwaukee, Wisconsin

Milwaukee is Wisconsin's largest city. Many German immigrants settled in Milwaukee during the 1840s and today the city still has a large German-American population. Milwaukee hosts so many ethnic and cultural events that the city has taken the nickname "City of Festivals." These events include the Asian Moon Festival, Polish Fest, Bastille Days, Festa Italiana, and the African World Festival. Most famous, though, is Milwaukee's Summerfest, the world's largest music festival.

Cleveland, Ohio

Cleveland is built where the Cuyahoga River flows into Lake Erie. Cleveland grew quickly to become the fifth largest U.S. city by 1920, but after the 1950s the city faced difficult economic times. Most recently Cleveland has become a leading center for health care and health sciences.

Ambassador Bridge

The Ambassador Bridge spans the Detroit River and connects Detroit to Windsor, Ontario, in Canada. Twenty-five percent of all merchandise trade between the United States and Canada crosses this bridge, making it the busiest international border crossing in North America.

Millions of cars and trucks cross the Ambassador Bridge each year.

Smaller cities

Although Chicago gets a lot of attention, there are hundreds of exciting small cities and towns throughout the Midwest. Each of these smaller cities offers a uniquely Midwestern experience.

One example is Madison, the capital of Wisconsin. Often called "The City of Four Lakes," Madison is built on an **isthmus** between Lake Mendota and Lake Monona, with Lakes Wingra and Waubesa nearby. With a rich cultural life and a booming economy, Madison has been ranked by *Money* magazine as one of the ten best U.S. cities in which to live.

Madison's Capitol is one of the key landmarks of the city.

Toledo, Ohio

Toledo, in northern Ohio on the shore of Lake Erie, is so closely connected to the glass industry that it is known as "Glass City." Toledo has been home to glass manufacturing of all kinds, including bottles, windows, windshields, and construction materials. In 1936 Toledo became the site of the first building completely covered in glass.

Omaha, Nebraska

Omaha, the largest city in Nebraska, was founded in 1854. Omaha is located on the Missouri River, across from Council Bluffs, Iowa. In the 1860s, Omaha became an important link in the first transcontinental railroad, which connected the railroads of the eastern United States to those of the Pacific Coast. Omaha grew rapidly as the center of the meatpacking industry and became home to many European immigrants who came to work in the slaughterhouses.

The main dome of the Iowa State Capitol in Des Moines is gilded with very thin sheets of gold. It shines brightly in the sun.

Rural Life

Moving to big cities

The Midwest has experienced a huge fall in its rural population. As people have moved from rural areas to cities and towns, the rural Midwest has lost one-third of its population since 1920. Some parts of the Midwest have fewer than two people per square mile (2.6 square kilometers), and there are more than 6,000 ghost towns in Kansas alone.

Farming has been part of Midwestern life since the first settlers arrived. For many years, farms were family businesses, with each member of the family contributing to the work of the farm. Recently though, that has changed, as large commercial farms have begun to move into the region.

The Midwest leads the nation in production of many different crops and livestock. Iowa is the nation's largest pig producer. More soybeans are grown in Illinois than anywhere else in the United States. Michigan grows 75 percent of the nation's tart cherries. Nebraska is one of the largest producers of beef cattle. Wisconsin produces 35 percent of all the cheese made in the United States, more than any other state.

Dairy cattle are a common sight in Wisconsin, while beef cattle graze on the mixed-grass prairies of Kansas and Nebraska.

Farming tools and technology

The success of farming in this region was made possible due to farming technology. After the invention of the steel plow in 1847, farmers had a new tool to help them even more starting in 1868: the steam tractor. Gas-powered tractors were introduced in 1910. By 1954 the number of tractors on farms exceeded the number of horses for the first time.

Farm machinery producers such as John Deere and International Harvester helped farming to succeed in the Midwest.

Fact file

Modern farming tractors are a big investment. One tractor can cost $150,000!

A tractor harvests soybeans and unloads them in a waiting truck.

Getting Around

Whether you go by boat, train, car, or plane, the Midwest is an easy place in which to travel. The Midwest's central location in the United States makes it easy to get from here to almost anywhere else in the country.

Rivers and canals were important routes for transportation in the early days of the Midwest, but the arrival of railroads brought enormous growth and change to the region. As railroads connected the East Coast of the United States to the West, the Midwest became the transportation hub of the country. Anybody or anything traveling from one side of the country to the other had to come through the Midwest.

Go by boat

Barges have been in use on the Mississippi River for nearly 200 years. Even today, when modern freight trains and semi-trailers are available, shipping goods by river barge is still the cheapest method of transportation. Modern river barges are nearly 1200 feet (366 meters) in length. Barges are held together with steel cables and pushed by towboats.

Huge barges move goods up and down the Mississippi River. More grain travels ▶ on the Mississippi than any other river system in the world.

Midwestern roads

The best way to see the Midwest is by car. The many interstate highways, state highways, and local roads that crisscross the region make it possible to travel from Ohio to Nebraska in a couple of days, a trip that would have taken early settlers months to complete.

Two of the most famous highways in the United States are part of the Midwest highway system. Historic Route 66, built in 1926 and no longer a highway since 1985, began in Chicago and traveled through Illinois, Missouri, and Kansas on its way to Los Angeles, California. The Lincoln Highway, the first **transcontinental** highway in America, passes through Ohio, Indiana, Illinois, Iowa, and Nebraska, following the route of U.S. Highway 30.

Mackinac Bridge

The Mackinac Bridge connects Michigan's Lower Peninsula to the Upper Peninsula across the Straits of Mackinac, where Lake Michigan meets Lake Huron. Stretching for five miles (eight kilometers) across open water, the Mackinac Bridge is one of the world's largest suspension bridges. On Labor Day each year, the bridge is closed to vehicle traffic for the Mackinac Bridge Walk.

The Mackinac Bridge opened in 1957 and since then more than 100 million vehicles have crossed it.

Work in the Area

There are many different kinds of jobs and businesses that keep Midwestern cities thriving. Chicago is the financial center of the Midwest. Omaha, Nebraska, is home to 30 insurance companies and more than 24 telemarketing companies. Indianapolis, Indiana, and St. Louis, Missouri, have both attracted a growing number of high-technology companies. Kansas leads the nation in building airplanes for both business and military use.

Some of the country's largest companies are headquartered in the Midwest, including car manufacturers such as the General Motors Corporation in Detroit, Michigan, and the Ford Motor Company in nearby Dearborn.

The Ford Motor Company's River Rouge Plant in Dearborn, Michigan, was built between 1915 and 1927. It was the first automobile plant to include nearly every aspect of automobile manufacturing in a single place.

The Chicago Board of Trade

The Chicago Board of Trade (CBOT) was founded in 1848 to serve as a central marketplace for buying and selling crops, such as corn, wheat, and oats. This allowed farmers to know in advance what sort of price they might get for their crops.

For more than 150 years, members of the CBOT traded face-to-face in the trading pits, buying and selling contracts for agricultural products. Now much of the trading happens electronically, and the CBOT trades many financial products, in addition to the original agricultural products.

John H. Johnson

John H. Johnson attended the University of Chicago and Northwestern University in Illinois. In 1942 he borrowed $500 to start publishing his first magazine. Johnson Publishing later became the largest African-American owned publishing company in the world. Johnson Publishing is best known for the magazines *Ebony*, founded in 1945, and *Jet*, first published in 1951. In these and other magazines, Johnson's goal was to create a positive media image for all African Americans.

◄ Airplanes are constructed inside the Boeing Company plant in Wichita, Kansas.

37

Cereal centers

In 1898 Dr. John Kellogg and his brother Will invented flaked corn cereal for their health spa in Battle Creek, Michigan. Today, cereal makers are dotted throughout the Midwest. In Iowa Quaker Oats operates the largest cereal processing plant in the country. Kellogg's is still headquartered in Battle Creek, Michigan. The headquarters of General Mills is located in Golden Valley, Minnesota.

Glorious food

Much of the food sold throughout the United States is grown, produced, or packed in the Midwest. This is why the Midwest has been called the nation's "breadbasket."

Many of the Midwestern states are involved in food processing. Meatpacking is one of Nebraska's main businesses. Minnesota is home to food-processing companies such as General Mills, Land O' Lakes, Pillsbury, and Hormel. Kraft Foods is headquartered in Northfield, Illinois, a suburb of Chicago.

Kellogg's Cereal City, in Battle Creek, Michigan, is a museum, factory tour, and breakfast-cereal theme park, all in one.

38

Steel industry

Much of the steel that was used to build the railroads and skyscrapers throughout the United States was mined and milled in the Midwest. The steel mills of Indiana were vital to the growth of many industries from the middle of the 1800s to the late 1900s.

The steel produced in the Midwest was used to build cars in the automobile plants of Michigan, and to manufacture farm machinery in Illinois and throughout the United States. In the second half of the 1900s, though, there was a sharp decline in the need for steel. That and a slump in the auto market hurt job opportunities for steelworkers in Indiana and Michigan badly.

Iron ore is mined in many places throughout the Midwest, including Minnesota, where this truck is being loaded with the ore to take away for processing.

Treasure in the ground

Mining has long been an important part of the Midwest economy, but people did not mine metals like gold and silver here. Instead, these mines contain iron, coal, sand, gravel, salt, and limestone. Ohio has the deepest salt mine in the country, at 2,000 feet (610 meters). In Kansas, one salt mine is also used to store important documents, pictures, and film. The temperature and humidity in the mine are perfect for preserving old materials. In fact, the original film negatives of *The Wizard of Oz* and *Gone With the Wind* are stored there!

Free Time

Museums are common throughout the Midwest. In fact Detroit, Kansas City, Chicago, Milwaukee, Minneapolis, and Cleveland all have world-class art museums. Sculpture displayed in public places is also common in the Midwest. For example, the Minneapolis Sculpture Garden features more than 40 permanent works by leading American and international artists.

In Chicago, the Art Institute, the Field Museum of Natural History, the John G. Shedd Aquarium, and the Adler Planetarium are just a short walk from one another. Milwaukee's Art Museum, on the Lake Michigan waterfront, features a remarkable addition designed by architect Santiago Calitrava.

Children's Theater Company

This unique and award-winning theater company in Minneapolis, Minnesota, focuses solely on plays for children. More than 6 million children and families have attended performances by the Children's Theater Company since it was founded in 1965.

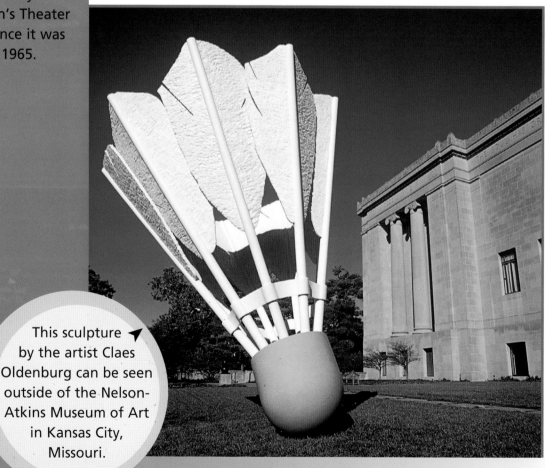

This sculpture by the artist Claes Oldenburg can be seen outside of the Nelson-Atkins Museum of Art in Kansas City, Missouri.

Jazz and blues

Jazz and blues music have a special place in the Midwest cities of Kansas City, St. Louis, and Chicago. Although both jazz and blues first developed in the South, especially New Orleans, they were popularized in these Midwestern cities during the first half of the 1900s. The American Jazz Museum is based in Kansas City.

Country music

The town of Branson in southern Missouri has become a center for country and bluegrass music. Visitors from all over the country come to Branson for music, comedy, and variety shows.

Motown sound

In 1959 songwriter Berry Gordy started a record label that he called "Motown," named after the city in which he lived: Detroit, the Motor City. Motown became the first record label owned by an African American to achieve international success. Some of Motown's most famous artists include Marvin Gaye, The Supremes, The Temptations, Stevie Wonder, and the Jackson 5.

The "wings" on the roof of the Milwaukee Art Museum can open and close.

Taste of the Midwest

The Midwestern menu has just about anything you'd want to eat, from Chicago-style pizza to a spinach milkshake at the Lenexa, Kansas, Spinach Festival. Sausages are a popular food in the Midwest. For almost a century, Detroiters have been buying hot dogs from two landmark restaurants in downtown Detroit— American Coney Island and Lafayette Coney Island. The way to serve a hot dog in Detroit is with chopped onions, chili, and yellow mustard only.

Cincinnati considers itself the chili capital of the world. Legend says that the unique Cincinnati Five-Way Chili was invented by Greek immigrants in the early 1900s. It's called "Five-Way" for the five major ingredients: beef, beans, onions, cheese, and spaghetti!

Popular popcorn

Americans eat 17 billion quarts (about 16 billion liters) of popcorn each year, and most of it comes from the Midwest, with Indiana and Nebraska producing the most popcorn. Marion, Ohio, is home to the Wyandot Popcorn Museum and an annual Popcorn Festival held in September.

Chicago-style pizza usually features a deep, thick crust. ▶

Barbecues and boils

Kansas City residents claim that their unique style of barbecue is the best in the country. The distinctive taste and texture of Kansas City barbecue sauce comes from the mixture of vinegar, tomato sauce, hot pepper, and molasses.

The recipe for a Door County fish boil originated with the Scandinavian settlers and lumberjacks who settled the Northwoods of Wisconsin. Fresh whitefish, potatoes, and onions are boiled in a large pot over an open fire. When the meal is cooked, the pot is allowed to boil over, extinguishing the flames in a cloud of steam.

A Door County fish boil is not just good food; it's a fiery show! ◀

The first ice cream cone

Legend has it that the ice cream cone was invented on a hot summer day at the St. Louis World's Fair in 1904. According to one story, an ice cream vendor and a waffle salesman teamed up to create the first ice cream cone. In fact, ice cream cones had probably been around for many years, but the St. Louis World's Fair definitely made them a popular treat.

Wrigley Field

Wrigley Field, home of the Chicago Cubs baseball team, was built in 1914. It is the second oldest baseball field in the United States, and the first to use organ music to help entertain fans. Wrigley Field was nicknamed "The Friendly Confines" by former Cub and Hall of Famer Ernie Banks, and the park is known for its ivy-covered outfield walls.

Good sports

Midwesterners take their sports seriously, both professional and college athletics. Baseball, basketball, football, and hockey are all big winners. Kansas, Nebraska, and Iowa have no professional teams, but fans of college sports in those states have plenty to cheer about. Two Ohio cities, Cleveland and Cincinnati, each have their own teams.

One of the most popular events in the Midwest is the Indy 500 auto race. Each Memorial Day, the Indianapolis Speedway hosts this famous auto racing event. Cars race 500 miles (804 kilometers) in 200 laps. The Speedway was built in 1909 to test and race new cars, and the first race was held in 1911. The track is often called the Brickyard because it was originally paved with bricks.

The Indy 500 in Indianapolis, Indiana, is a popular sporting event in the Midwest.

The Big Ten

The Big Ten is the name of the oldest college athletic **conference** in the United States, even though there are actually eleven members. Ten of the Big Ten schools are in the Midwest (only Pennsylvania State University is not). The schools of the Big Ten compete in many sports, but football and basketball are the most popular.

High school basketball is a major sport in Indiana, the Hoosier state. For many years (until 1997), every high school basketball team in Indiana competed against every other team in the state basketball tournament. Residents and natives of Indiana nearly always call themselves Hoosiers. But no one knows exactly where or when the nickname began.

Olympic track star Jesse Owens grew up in Cleveland, Ohio.

Track star

Jesse Owens first began to run when he was picked for his track team at Fairview Junior High. A few years later, Jesse Owens won four gold medals in the 1936 Olympics. The 1936 Olympic Games were held in Nazi Germany when Adolf Hitler was dictator. Hitler wanted to prove to the world that the non-Jewish German race of people was superior. However, Owens stole the show. Even German fans cheered loudly for Owens as he won medal after medal, proving Hitler to be wrong.

Fact file
The Cincinnati Red Stockings (now just the Reds) is the oldest professional baseball team in America; they began playing in 1869.

A race on skis

Each winter since 1973, Wisconsin hosts the Birkebeiner Cross-Country Ski Marathon. More than 8,000 skiers from all over the world compete in different races of different lengths over three days. It is North America's largest cross-country ski race. The American Birkebeiner Race is named after a much older cross-country ski race in Norway.

Outdoor recreation

There are plenty of opportunities for outdoor activities in the Midwest. Along the Great Lakes are beautiful beaches, including the Indiana Dunes National Lakeshore and Sleeping Bear Dunes in Michigan. Each state has trails and roads to hike or bike, lakes in which to swim or fish, rivers to paddle, and woods for camping.

Fishing is popular in nearly every Midwest state. Almost half of all Minnesotans buy a fishing license each year, and they keep on fishing, even when the lakes are frozen! In order to go ice fishing, you find a lake with thick, strong ice, drive your car or truck right onto the frozen lake, set up your small shelter, cut a hole in the ice, and drop your line.

Cross-country skiers are elbow to elbow at the start of the Birkebeiner Race.

Fact file

Every state in the Midwest has its own system of state parks, but Michigan has the most, with 97 state parks.

Boating

The thousands of lakes and rivers throughout the Midwest provide plentiful opportunities for boating, whether your boat moves by paddle, sail, or motor. Lake of the Ozarks in Missouri has nearly 1,300 miles (2,092 kilometers) of coastline, more coastline than the state of California!

The Boundary Waters Canoe Area Wilderness, at the border of Minnesota and Canada, is a beautiful network of wild rivers and lakes.

In the Boundary Waters, paddle power is the only way to get around, since motorboats are not allowed in most of the area.

RAGBRAI

Each summer since 1973, the Des Moines Register newspaper has hosted the Register's Annual Great Bicycle Race Across Iowa (RAGBRAI). In this five-day event, 10,000 riders from all over the state and beyond bike from one end of Iowa to the other.

Cyclists from around the world participate in RAGBRAI.

National Cherry Festival

Since 1926, Traverse City, Michigan, has hosted the National Cherry Festival. This event celebrates and promotes the little red fruit for which Michigan is famous. Michigan is home to many sour cherry orchards, and Traverse City has proclaimed itself Cherry Capital of the World. The Cherry Festival features parades, music, contests, and every sort of cherry-filled treat you can imagine.

Festivals

Everywhere you go in the Midwest, you will find unique and interesting places, activities, and events. Every state has its collection of unusual festivals. These include the Red Flannel Festival in Cedar Springs, Michigan; Prairie Days, in Independence, Kansas; Lumberjack Days in Stillwater, Minnesota; Twins Day Festival in Twinsburg, Ohio; and a host of ethnic events such as Nordic Fest, Finnish Fest, Danish Fest, and Irish Fest.

Every September, Chesterton, Indiana, holds an enormous Wizard of Oz Festival. In January of each year, St. Paul, Minnesota, hosts the oldest and largest winter carnival in the United States. It features cultural celebrations, parades, contests, snow sculpting, and an ice palace.

An ice sculptor prepares a piece for a competition at the St. Paul Winter Carnival.

Making amusement

Amusement parks can be found throughout the Midwest. Cedar Point Amusement Park in Sandusky, Ohio, contains sixteen roller coasters, the largest cluster of them in the world. Cedar Point contains 47,353 feet (14,433 meters) of roller coaster track! The Mall of America in Minnesota even has an indoor amusement park. The Mall of America is the largest indoor mall in the world, with 520 stores.

In central Wisconsin, the Wisconsin River flows through remarkable gorges and rock formations formed in the sandstone cliffs and banks. This area, called the Wisconsin Dells, offers both natural beauty and a remarkable number of water parks. It is a popular tourist destination for people living in the Midwest and beyond.

Circus World Museum

In the late 1800s, Wisconsin became known as the "mother of circuses," because so many circuses started there or spent winters in the state. The famous Ringling Bros. Circus was founded in Wisconsin. Today, the Circus World Museum is located in Baraboo, Wisconsin.

The strange and beautiful rock formations in the Dells of the Wisconsin River are the result of floods that took place 19,000 years ago.

An Amazing Region

For thousands of years, diverse cultures flourished in the lands we now call the Midwest. Although people have lived in the Midwest for thousands of years, for the past 220 years the land has been reshaped into farms, cities, and large suburbs. The growth of the Midwest during the past 200 years was fueled by the rich resources of the region.

The Midwest has experienced many changes, and the future holds even more. Cities that grew rapidly in the past must now find new ways to keep their residents from moving away. Manufacturing regions must find ways to clean up pollution left from closed factories. Growing suburbs must find ways to use land and resources wisely.

Purest English

The accent, or way a person speaks, of someone who grew up in the Midwest is often thought to be the purest example of "standard" American English. This is one reason why some famous television broadcasters are from the Midwest. Many famous television broadcasters and show hosts including David Letterman, Tom Brokaw, and Johnny Carson have come from the Midwest.

This sculpture, called "Spoonbridge and Cherry," is a popular attraction in the Minneapolis Sculpture Garden. Behind it is the Minneapolis skyline. ◀

Land of promise

The Midwest is full of surprises and contrasts, small towns and big cities, open prairies and towering skyscrapers, rolling farmland and the Great Lakes. Midwesterners face many challenges. Growing city and suburban populations, dwindling rural populations, changing job opportunities, and changing ecosystems all affect Midwesterners. Even so, wherever you go in the Midwest region, you'll find interesting people, a warm welcome, and plenty of fun things to see and do.

The Lake Erie Islands are popular summer destinations, not far from the shores of Sandusky, Ohio.

Rolling, green farms will always be an important part of the Midwest. The Midwest is an important link in the world's food supply chain.

Science at work

Scientists are hard at work on the future of **physics** at Fermilab National Accelerator Laboratory, just outside of Chicago. Over the last 40 years, thousands of scientists have used Fermilab's high-technology tools for experiments in high-energy physics. Fermilab is home to several machines that allow scientists to smash open atoms and study the smallest pieces of the universe.

Find Out More

World Wide Web

The Fifty States
www.infoplease.com/
states.html

This website has a clickable U.S. map that gives facts about each of the 50 states, plus images of state flags.

These sites have pictures, statistics, and other facts about each state in the Midwest:

Enjoy Illinois
www.enjoyillinois.com/

Enjoy Indiana
www.in.gov/enjoyindiana/

Explore Minnesota
www.exploreminnesota.com/

Iowa
www.iowa.gov

Kansas
www.travelks.com/

Michigan
www.michigan.org/

Missouri
www.visitmo.com/

Nebraska
www.visitnebraska.org/

Ohio
www.ohio.gov

Wisconsin
www.travelwisconsin.com/

Books to read

Brink, Carol Ryrie. *Caddie Woodlawn*. Thorndike, ME: Thorndike Press, 2003.

Doherty, Kieran. *Voyageurs, Lumberjacks, and Farmers: Pioneers of the Midwest*. Minneapolis, Minn.: Oliver Press, 2003.

Jackson, Robert. *Meet Me in St. Louis: A Trip to the 1904 World's Fair*. New York, NY: HarperCollins, 2004.

Mirocha, Paul, Sara St. Antoine, and Trudy Nicholson. *The Great Lakes: Stories from Where We Live*. Minneapolis, Minn.: Milkweed Editions, 2005.

Places to visit

Art Institute of Chicago (Chicago, Illinois)
This museum has an extensive collection of art and artifacts from around the world.

Henry Ford Museum and Greenfield Village (Dearborn, Michigan)
This is the largest indoor/outdoor museum in the country.

Old World Wisconsin (Eagle, Wisconsin)
This living history museum contains 60 original structures from all over Wisconsin.

Wisconsin Dells (north of Baraboo, Wisconsin)
Sandstone cliffs and rock formations as well as numerous waterparks can be found in the area.

Timeline

1000 B.C.
Adena people first arrive in the Midwest.

100 B.C.
Hopewell people first arrive in the Midwest.

A.D. 1671
French build Fort Michilimackinac on the southern shore of the Straits of Mackinac.

1763
French and Indian War ends.

1763
Wisconsin becomes part of British territory.

1775
American Revolution begins.

1783
Colonies gain independence from Great Britain.

1796
American troops occupy forts at Detroit and Mackinac.

1857
U.S. Supreme Court declares Dred Scott must remain a slave.

1854
Nebraska Territory created by the Kansas-Nebraska Act.

1841
First wagon trains leave Independence, Missouri, to travel the Oregon Trail.

1830
Congress passes the Indian Removal Act.

1811
New Madrid earthquake, centered near New Madrid, Missouri is the second worst known earthquake in the United States.

1804
Meriwether Lewis and William Clark leave St. Louis to explore the Louisiana Purchase.

1803
The United States makes the Louisiana Purchase.

1861-1865
U.S. Civil War takes place.

1862
Congress passes the Homestead Act.

1871
Great Chicago Fire destroys much of Chicago, Illinois.

1884
Ringling Brothers Circus founded in Baraboo, Wisconsin.

1893
World's Columbian Exposition is held in Chicago.

1894
Kellogg Brothers makes first wheat flakes, in Battle Creek, Michigan.

1903
Ford Motor Company is created.

1904
St. Louis hosts a world's fair.

1993
Severe flooding occurs along upper Mississippi River.

1973
Sears Tower is completed in Chicago, Illinois.

1965
Gateway Arch is completed in St. Louis, Missouri.

1959
St. Lawrence Seaway opens, allowing ships to pass from the Atlantic Ocean into the Great Lakes.

1934–35
Years of drought lead to the Dust Bowl; thousands of families leave their land and travel west.

1929
Stock market crash and beginning of the Great Depression.

1911
First Indianapolis 500 Auto Race.

States at a Glance

Illinois
Nicknames: Land of Lincoln; The Prairie State
Became State: 1818
Capital: Springfield
Motto: State Sovereignty, National Union
Flower: Violet
Animal: White-tailed Deer
Song: "Illinois"

Indiana
Nickname: The Hoosier State
Became State: 1816
Capital: Indianapolis
Motto: Crossroads of America
Flower: Peony
Song: "On the Banks of the Wabash, Far Away"

Iowa
Nickname: The Hawkeye State
Became State: 1846
Capital: Des Moines
Motto: Our Liberties We Prize, and Our Rights We Will Maintain
Flower: Wild Rose
Song: "The Song of Iowa"

Kansas
Nickname: The Sunflower State
Became State: 1861
Capital: Topeka
Motto: To the Stars through Difficulties
Flower: Sunflower
Animal: Buffalo
Song: "Home on the Range"

Michigan
Nicknames: The Wolverine State: The Great Lakes State
Became State: 1837
Capital: Lansing
Motto: If You Seek a Pleasant Peninsula, Look About You
Flower: Apple blossom
Animal: White-tailed deer
Song: "Michigan, My Michigan"

Minnesota
Nicknames: : North Star State; The Land of 10,000 Lakes; The Gopher State
Became State: 1858
Capital: Saint Paul
Motto: *L'etoile du Nord* (Star of the North)
Flower: Pink and white lady slipper
Song: "Hail! Minnesota"

Missouri
Nickname: The Show Me State
Became State: 1821
Capital: Jefferson City
Motto: The Welfare of the People Shall be the Supreme Law
Flower: Hawthorn
Animal: Missouri Mule
Song: "The Missouri Waltz"

Nebraska
Nickname: The Cornhusker State
Became State: 1867
Capital: Lincoln
Motto: Equality Before the Law
Flower: Goldenrod
Animal: White-tailed deer
Song: "Beautiful Nebraska"

Ohio
Nickname: The Buckeye State
Became State: 1803
Capital: Columbus
Motto: With God, All Things Are Possible
Flower: Scarlet carnation
Animal: White-tailed deer
Song: "Beautiful Ohio"

Wisconsin
Nickname: Badger State
Became State: 1848
Capital: Madison
Motto: Forward
Flower: Wood violet
Animal: Badger
Song: "On, Wisconsin!"

Glossary

American Revolution war fought from 1775 to 1783 between Great Britain and the colonies in America that resulted in independence for the United States

archeologist person who studies past human life

border dividing line between one country or region and another

commercial something done or created for money

Confederacy the states of Alabama, Arkansas, Florida, Georgia, Louisiana, Mississippi, North Carolina, South Carolina, and Tennessee during the Civil War

conference group of sports teams that play each other

culture customs, language, art, and ideas shared by a group of people

drought long period of time when there is no rain

ecosystem complex community of plants and animals living in a certain place

endangered threatened

flyway route followed by migrating birds

glacier thick, slow-moving sheet of ice

habitat place where a person or animal lives

Homestead Act law passed in the 1860s whereby settlers could claim 160 acres of land if they built a house, planted crops, and stayed for five years

homesteaders people who were given public land for building a home

hub center

immigrants people who leave their country to settle in another

irrigation the transport of water to land

isthmus narrow strip of land with water on both sides

legislator member of the government who helps make laws

limestone type of rock often used as a building material

Louisiana Purchase agreement signed in 1803 in which the United States bought France's land in North America

metropolitan area area that includes a city and the suburbs around it

mica kind of rock that can be split apart into thin sheets

physics science of matter, space, and time

pioneers first people to settle in a new place

plateau high, flat area of land

sod piece of soil held together by roots and grass

transcontinental across the entire continent

Underground Railroad network of safe places set up by people who helped runaway slaves

Union name for the United States during the Civil War that referred to the states not in the Confederacy

wetland low-lying land with few or no trees

Index